TICKLED PINK

TICKLED PINK

A COLLECTION OF FOUR-LINE VERSE

Helen Seeley Phillips

Foreword by Rachel Sauer

Ⴔ

PRECISION CREATIVE PRESS

DENVER, COLORADO

Illustrations by HavanaStreet.com

Precision Creative Press
P.O. Box 440502
Denver, Colorado 80044
www.precisioncreative.com

First Paperback Edition February 2007

Includes material previously published in
*Capper's Weekly, Good Housekeeping, Mature Living, Grit,
Ohio Motorist, The Saturday Evening Post, The Wall Street Journal.*

Library of Congress Control Number: 2007922702

ISBN 978-0-6151-4057-5

For Boyd

Foreword

by Rachel Sauer

It's very subtle, how she does it, but Helen Phillips' writing fingers are always moving — on the tablecloth after dinner, on the arm of her chair, even on her knee if her hands are in her lap.

It's an unconscious habit. With her invisible pen — or just with her fingernail, if the pen's out of ink — she transcribes snippets of conversation she just heard, or a witty comment someone just made. She does it even as she talks and laughs, and anyone who's enjoyed a meal or a meandering conversation with her knows about this endearing habit. Mostly, she's not aware she's doing it until someone asks her what she's writing and she laughs and shrugs.

Sometimes, though, she grows quiet and contemplative, considering the words before she writes them. In those times, I watch her write and I wonder, "What is she writing?"

Helen Phillips is a writer. It's who she is and writing is what she loves. Talk with her for just five minutes and you'll know that she relishes language, with its layers and nuance and flexibility. Even more, she loves a good story. Put them together, and her path as a writer emerges — from whimsical poems and essays to mystery novels.

Once I went with her to a writers' group meeting and listened to her volley ideas with the other women there. I remember her reading a phrase out loud, then adjusting the wording and asking, "Doesn't that sound better?" And it really did. She knows what will nudge a reader along.

I became a writer in part because my grandmother set such an interesting example. I've always heard that true writers write because they must, because they wake up thinking about it. Some days, I think the only reason I do it is because I'd get fired if I didn't. But in those moments, if I'm especially lucky, I hear Gram's voice asking, "Doesn't that sound better?" Then I remember that words are exciting, and putting them together into stories is so much fun.

Gram taught me that.

Introduction

Light verse is a poetic style intended to be light-hearted and humorous. In this collection, each verse is limited to just four lines. Yet, despite the seeming simplicity, often a deeper meaning lies just below the surface.

The challenge of light verse is to take a point of fact and manipulate it into something which makes you smile or chuckle while at the same time nodding your head in agreement. Always clever, sometimes silly, often wry, and at times poignant, each verse stands as a snapshot image of a true moment in life.

Finding the best word, the most succinct expression, the right juxtaposition…therein lies the art.

TICKLED PINK

Lighter Side

Sometimes sly wit and humor
Can make one stop and think;
Just take things one smile further
And end up tickled pink.

Beginnings

The passing years remind us
It's best for all to know,
Life not only begins at 40
It also begins to show.

Never Fails

One of life's early lessons
Is sadly all too true:
Success occurs in private
And failure in full view.

Boyd's Favorite

The test of spring housecleaning
Is one I seldom flunk.
I sort and save <u>my</u> treasures
And eliminate <u>his</u> junk.

Vacation Dreams

Dad yearns for mountain trails to hike,
Mom opts for sun and sand;
Their offspring vie to break the tie:
All go to Disneyland.

Weather Report

Weathering the storms of life
Is mostly what it takes
Life's really like a snowstorm
You encounter a lot of flakes.

Dog Daze

One question I have pondered,
I'd like to get it right:
If every doggie has his day
Why do some bark all night?

Money's Worth

There's this about
Most free advice:
It's more than likely
Worth the price.

Procrastination

Life teaches many lessons,
Some by the sweat of your brow.
Hard work pays off in the future,
Laziness pays off now.

Yes and No

A lot of life's problems
Are quite easy to rate:
Saying yes too early
And saying no too late.

Reminder

If grandkids you're indulging
Means credit cards start maxing,
The kids may be deductible
But sometimes they are taxing.

Reach Out

Make helping others
Your signature style
It's never too crowded
On that extra mile.

No Second Chance

Pay heed to ancient maxims
But know this to be true:
If at first you don't succeed
Skydiving is not for you.

Money Wise

If you're down on your luck
And it's ready money you lack,
Always borrow from a pessimist –
He won't expect it back.

Full Speed

Who says old age will slow you down?
Don't pay them any heed.
Just know that when you're over the hill
You'll begin to pick up speed.

Budget Woes

I'm working on my budget woes:
I messed things up a bit.
I finally got both ends to meet
And found they didn't fit.

Match Game

A single man who's footloose
Is not too easy to catch –
But any man with money to burn
Is sure to meet his match.

Ear Ache

In the car ahead
The sign was bold:
"It's NOT too loud,
You're just too old!"

True Friends

Good friends are like angels
Or an answer to prayer
You don't have to see them
To know they are there.

Decisions, Decisions

Decisions are a pain to make,
Few come without a hitch;
If we could market afterthoughts
Perhaps we'd all be rich!

Rebel

I'm up to here with scrubbing,
The dusting is left to chance.
My new idea of housework
Is to sweep a room with a glance.

Cry Foul

I have made astute decisions
Firm and forthright, no retreat;
Then I stood up to be counted
And somebody took my seat.

Check It Out

If you've got your groove back
And your life begins to thrill,
When the going seems too easy
Maybe you're going downhill.

Staying Power

Heed, O prospective houseguests
If a gracious host you seek:
Some people stay longer in one hour
Than others do in a week.

Look Ahead

Remember this
If hope has died:
At the lowest ebb
Comes the turn of the tide.

Plan Ahead

In contemplating future goals
Don't let your planning fizzle.
Hard workers carve out great careers
While slackers simply chisel.

☙　☙　☙

Senior Moment

I was just warming up to my subject
With my verbal skills in full sway
When I suffered a brief Senior Moment
And forgot what I started to say.

Macho Traveler

He scans the maps and roadside signs,
Drives round and round forever;
Pretends to know the way to go –
But ask directions? Never!

Sure Cure

This thought comes unbidden
As I lie counting sheep:
The best cure for insomnia
Is to get a lot of sleep.

Hard Lesson

The years, alas, keep piling up
And leave just this to say:
I find there's almost nothing else
For me to learn the hard way.

Fuelish Lament

Conserving fuel
Is now our lot;
The cars get smaller
But I do not.

Friendship

To keep alive a friendship
New math you should employ,
Just divide up all the sorrow
And multiply the joy.

Happy Day

Our son has reached the perfect age
For which most parents strive:
He's old enough to shovel snow
But still too young to drive.

Just Looking, Thanks...

Whenever I'm "just looking"
Store clerks are everywhere.
But when I make my mind up —
They've vanished in thin air!

Socially Skilled

To elude that boring cohort
Quickly escape to the john,
But to make a long story short
Yawn.

Name Game

If seeking Mr. Right
Becomes a woman's game,
Best she make sure that "always"
Does not precede his name.

Loser's Lament

A diet is so endless!
If I were keeping score
I'd vow I've lost the same 10 pounds
A dozen times or more.

So They Say

Procrastination is so easy –
Moreover, you can bet
The longer you just put it off
The harder it will get.

Traffic Trauma

When time is of the essence
With deadlines I can't miss,
Why is traffic so congested
Andallbackeduplikethis?

Bounce Back

In assessing your problems
One adage still counts —
The harder you fall
The higher you bounce.

Financial Wizardry

To safely double your money
Here's good advice – don't knock it!
Just fold it over once
And put it in your pocket.

Time of Change

Time brought a change in my lifestyle
To clean up my act was a must.
Now four letter words are a no-no,
Like wash, iron, cook and dust.

Ho Hum

Assessment of life's ups and downs
Tells me to rise above it.
Yet – I'll admit I've seen it all
And didn't think much of it.

Auto-Motive

If life's like an auto,
One rule should be clear:
Never start your mouth
Until your brain's in gear.

Cheap Talk

Some claim that talk is cheap –
They're right, of course, until
The postman makes his daily rounds
And leaves your telephone bill.

Timeless

The planes and trains you aim for
By some odd quirk of fate
Are late when you get there early
And on time when you're running late.

Fashion Plate

I added to my wardrobe,
A major fashion fling.
When someone said, "new dress?"
Replied, "Oh, this old thing."

No Problem

It's no problem to be nifty
When you're 50,
But much harder to be frisky
When you're 60.

Quitters

He boasts that he's a self-made man,
It's quite an ego boon;
But those who know him best agree
He quit the job too soon.

Face It

Just keep looking on the bright side,
Don't make mountains out of hills;
There are bigger things than money
And the biggest one is bills.

Changeless

Facing up to changing shape
Is now my life's endeavor;
Brain cells come and brain cells go
But fat cells live forever.

Sweet Success

If finishing the task at hand
Should leave you feeling dazed,
And if at first you <u>do</u> succeed
Try not to look amazed.

Be Thankful

When aches and pains take over
And the ills of age are lurking,
Most days I can be grateful
At least my tongue's still working.

Checkmate

I case the check-out counter
Then make a note of time;
Too late! The line that's moving
Is not the one where I'm.

Don't Count Me Out

My gait's a bit slower,
Though I'm feeling fine.
I'm not over the hill,
I'm just on the back nine.

A Good Life

A good life is not measured,
At least that's what they say,
By the total number of breaths we take
But by those that take our breath away.

New Direction

I hesitated on the doorstep
My mind assailed with doubt.
When I paused upon the threshold
Was I coming in or going out?

Survive the Drive

When I'm tied up in traffic
There's one thing I'd like to know:
Why do they call it rush hour
When traffic is stop and go?

Motel Musings

Why is the noisy traveler
Who hits the road at four
With talk and raucous laughter
Forever right next door?

☙ ☙ ☙

April Lament

Budgets are red
Husbands are blue
Tempers are short —
Taxes are due.

Timely Education

When our son went off to college,
Much advice was quickly spurned;
Now we notice, four years later,
He's impressed with all we've learned!

The New Latin

Think back to Latin studies
And how they kept us hopping.
Now Vini, Vidi, Visa means
"I came, I saw, went shopping."

Secrets

The way to be happy
Is easy to see
Have a good sense of humor
And a bad memory.

Nostalgia

Think back to the days we call olden,
When earning a dollar took brawn;
Our worries were "Where will it come from?"
And not, "Good grief, where has it gone?"

After All

After all
Is said and done
Too much is said
And not enough done.

Night Owl

I used to be such a night owl
Ignoring the sleep I would lose
So why is it now such a struggle
To last till the 10 o'clock news?

Opportunity Knocks

This sermon from the ancients
Can make you feel remiss!
Opportunities are never lost
Someone grabs those you miss.

Selective Memory

It's hard to admit
That, obviously,
The older I get
The better I used to be!

Pattern for Success

Forgiveness takes effort
But you'll find, in the end,
You'll eliminate your enemy
When you make him your friend.

Sage Advice

Old sayings come to mind
Some even short and snappy
Like claiming ignorance is bliss
So why aren't more people happy?

Coming Up With Answers

Let the parents of our children
Be divided over rules,
But long as kids have tests to take
There'll be prayer in public schools.

Eye Opener

My wake-up call
Comes with two warnings:
I can open my eyes
But I don't do mornings.

Acting Up

You'll find that getting older
Is strictly for the birds.
Moving about is harder,
Actions creak louder than words.

Tassel Hassel

Graduation:

A confirmation of matriculation.

Is the tassel

Worth the hassel?

Poor Me

"A penny saved is a penny earned"
Easy for Franklin to say;
Who can name what a penny will buy
In the frenetic world today?

High School Reunion

All hail to the high school reunion!
That nostalgic time of the heart
When old classmates gather together
To see who is falling apart.

Travel Tip

After years of observation
I've found this rule applies:
Never travel faster
Than your guardian angel flies.

Hooray

Let's give those New Years resolutions
One last cheer
Mine lasted almost two full months
This year.

Sportsmanship

In a world of competition
Where the winners always move it,
You may think you'll be a good sport
But you have to lose to prove it.

Trial Run

The trials of life are many
To which mankind is prone:
Laugh and the world laughs with you,
Snore and you sleep alone.

All Due Credit

Don't give conscience all the credit
When you're tempted and retreat;
Many a halo being flaunted
Started out as two cold feet.

Never Too Old

To grow old gracefully
Is a most worthwhile endeavor.
You can only be young once,
But you can be immature forever.

Cover Up

There's no applause for losers,
To fail would dent your pride.
So if at first you don't succeed
Destroy all signs that you tried.

Always the Last Minute

Sometimes a busy lifestyle
Is not a lot of fun;
If it weren't for the last minute
Nothing would get done.

Rat Race

Competing in the rat race
You must remember that
No matter what the outcome,
The winner is still a rat.

Get Smart

Smarts come as one grows older.
Now passing years have shown,
Age doesn't always bring wisdom –
Sometimes age comes alone.

Nada

When nothing is the thing to do
Or nothing's left to say,
The wise forego the urge to quip
And thereby win the day.

Down Memory Lane

These days, I call up memories
For the pleasures they will bring;
Although it's hard to be nostalgic
When you can't remember a thing.

'Til You Drop

Did my Christmas shopping early,
Then let my pride prevail,
And after all was wrapped and given,
Saw all I'd bought…on sale.

Think Again

It's good to pause and ponder;
The brain needs rest, but then
Any time you stop to think –
Make sure you start again.

In All Modesty...

Comparing grandkids
Is where I shine,
Though it's obvious yours
Aren't as cute as mine!

Not Around Me You Don't

No smoking is the rule these days,
Though some can't squelch desire;
Its best to heed those warning signs
Since where there's smoke there's ire.

Q & A

I thought I knew all the answers
Back when I was younger and bolder;
How I wish I'd remember the questions
Now that I'm wiser and older.

❧   ❧   ❧

Dilemma

Where can I go
What can I say
To escape that pervasive
"Have a nice day!"

Prayer Power

There's this to keep in mind
As you wend along life's way:
If you're going to pray, don't worry.
If you're going to worry, why pray?

Climb On Up

Be not weary in well-doing
'Tho it's rest and solitude you seek;
If all life seems like uphill going
Perhaps it shows you've reached your peak.

Go Figure

In planning a lifetime together
Pay heed to the newlywed's song:
Two <u>can</u> live as cheaply as one
But only for half as long.

Vexation

Birthdays cause some contemplation
As the passing years unfold,
Face up to this one vexation:
We're too young to be this old!

Sleepy Time Gal

After a night that's restless
And spent in counting sheep,
Sometimes I wake up grumpy
And sometimes I let him sleep.

Quip Tease

That clever quip
You failed to say
Will come to mind
The following day.

Goodies

Holidays bring a time of cheer
With chances to indulge.
Reminding all to use restraint
In the battle of the bulge.

Shoulder to the Wheel

Some of life's lessons are painful
In spite of the best one can do.
Those who are smart cut wisdom teeth
Biting off more than they can chew.

Know-It-All

Try not to boast how smart you are –
It's really a solo affair.
Most people don't care how much you know
'Til they find out how much you care.

છ્ર   છ્ર   છ્ર

Kind Words

One thing really helps when you're building a life
It's sure to help you stand tall;
Just say something nice to the people you meet
Or don't say anything at all.

Play the Game

Life is like a football game
When you're in a goal line hunt.
Sometimes your side scores a touchdown,
But more often you have to punt.

Hit the Road

We are barely down the driveway,
Our vacation is all set,
When the back seat starts a chorus:
I'm starved! Are we there yet?

Amen

To stay the straight and narrow
Will keep your heart expanding,
And lots of kneeling, you will find,
Will keep you in good standing.

An Assist

Need a helping hand?
This works like a charm:
Try using the one
At the end of your arm.

Finish Line

When all sad words
Are said and done
The saddest are these:
"I should have won!"

Jackpot

"Big things coming your way"
My fortune cookie trills.
I was hoping for a jackpot,
But all I got was bills.

Mom's Relief

Those five little words
Weary moms find so cool
When summertime ends:
Hey kids! Back to school!

Speed Check

When taking care of business
One thing is sure to vex:
Bills travel thru the mail
At twice the speed of checks.

Always Thinking

In a social situation
Don't let questions go for naught.
If you don't have all the answers
You can offer food for thought.

The Highway

A difference of opinion
Is often hard to take.
Each time I try things your way
My head begins to ache.

An Odd Thing

Getting even with others
Is an easy thing to do.
Just make sure that getting even
Is always with those who've helped you.

Shopper's Lament

Although it seems, when shopping
That paying cash is rough,
The quickest way to lose your shirt
Is to put too much on the cuff.

Over and Over

There's one fact about growing old –
I find I really mean it.
One can watch an old TV rerun
And not remember having seen it.

Calm Down

When money woes assail us,
It doesn't help to fret;
An overload of worry
Won't pay an ounce of debt.

Memory

Wherever I go
Whatever I do
Memory's bright spot
Is thinking of you.

Mixed Signals

Twinkle, little traffic light,
Shining green both day and night.
When I approach you, having sped,
Why must you always turn to red?

Really Bugs Me

I really dislike,
Nay, have come to despise
Mosquitos, sandfleas,
Spiders, and flies.

Mindless

Hearing another viewpoint,
That's what it's all about.
I used to keep an open mind
Till my brains kept falling out.

Better To Give

Most of our possessions
We hang on to, you can bet;
Love's the only thing in this wide world
That you must give away to get.

Watching

It's nice to sit back
And enjoy all the funning.
Far cry from the days
When I hit the ground running!

Fine Whine

Bow your head
And moan aloud
Misery loves company
But prefers a crowd.

Easy Rider

Hush, little road rage,
Don't you cry.
You'll cause a car wreck
Bye and bye.

Solution

The man who can smile
When things go awry
Has gritted his teeth
And found a fall guy.

On Prayer

One way to make sure
Your prayers have wings:
Just pray for blessings
Instead of things.

Wisdom

In planning for your future
Let wisdom be the key:
Never grow a wishbone
Where a backbone ought to be.

Pause

Think what to say
Before you start
Since words are windows
To the heart.

Perspective

So often just the simple things
Can bring a world of hurt –
Making mountains out of molehills
Only takes a bit of dirt.

Rule of Thumb

This rule of thumb
Will take you far:
Trust in God
But lock your car.

Food For Thought

Life is not a bowl of cherries
No matter how you pick it;
It's really like an ice cream cone —
So go ahead and lick it!

Sleepytime Pal

One of life's problems
Occurs unrehearsed:
The person who snores
Always falls asleep first.

Index by Title

Index by Subject

About the Author

Helen Seeley Phillips has written books and many magazine articles. A lifelong resident of the Rocky Mountain West, she specializes in Juvenile Fiction, Western Non-fiction, and Light Verse.

She currently resides in Centennial, Colorado.

This book was set in Perpetua, a font designed in 1925 by Eric Gill for the Monotype foundry. Its distinctive style is based on monumental Roman inscriptions and old engravings.

Book design by Dennis Phillips

.

www.ingramcontent.com/pod-product-compliance
Lightning Source LLC
Chambersburg PA
CBHW031324040426
42443CB00005B/210